Time to get up

This book belongs to

_____

Written by Stephen Barnett
Illustrated by Rosie Brooks

Contents

Holiday fun 3

Running 13

Time to get up 21

New words 31

What did you learn? 32

About this book

Here are stories that will enlarge the child's understanding of the world, using characters, events and colourful illustrations to engage his or her interest and to introduce new words into their reading. Word lists at the end of the book will help the reader remember the new words they have been introduced to.

Holiday fun

We went to the beach for our holiday.

When we got there the sea had gone out. It was a long way to the water.

We took our things out of the car – the chairs, our towels and the picnic food.

The sea was still out.

We had our picnic lunch on the sand and fed the seagulls.

The sea was still out.

We made sand castles on the beach and dug holes.

But the sea was still out.

Then the sea came in!
The waves crashed on
the beach and we swam
and swam!

Running

Yesterday, mum gave me a new pair of running shoes. I like running.

I put the new shoes on,
and off I ran!

I ran

around the garden!

I ran

upstairs and downstairs!

I ran and ran until I could not run any more!

Time to get up

'Bringgg! Bringggg!' My alarm clock was ringing in the dark.

I put my hand out to switch it off. I was still a bit sleepy and it was hard to get out of bed.

This morning, I was getting up early to help my uncle milk the cows.

It was dark outside. I could see bright stars and the moon.

When I was dressed, my uncle and I walked to where the cows were waiting. I was warm in my coat, scarf and gumboots.

The cows were by the fence. We opened the gate so they could walk to the milking shed.

My uncle turned on the lights in the shed. We moved the cows inside.

After the cows had all been milked, we opened the gate to let them out.

Then we walked back to the house with a jug of milk for our breakfast.

New words

alarm	food	picnic
around	gate	ring
asleep	gumboot	running
beach	hand	sand
bed	holiday	scarf
breakfast	jug	shed
bright	later	shoes
castle	light	shut
chair	lunch	star
clock	milk	swam
coat	milking	thing
cow	moon	towel
dark	morning	turn
downstairs	move	uncle
dress	open	upstairs
early	outside	water
fence		yesterday

What did you learn?

Holiday fun
What things did the family take to the beach?
What is the colour of the car?
What did the children make in the sand?

Running
What is the colour of the running shoes?
Where does the girl run?

Time to get up
What time did the alarm clock start ringing?
What is the colour of the cows?
What did they take back to the house in the jug?